DRIVEN TO SUCCEED

With Unstoppable Motivation

7 Habits for Developing Deliberate Wealth

Dr. Titus C. Wright

Copyright 2019 Titus C. Wright

This publication may not be reproduced,
stored in a retrieval system or transmitted in
whole or in part, in any form or by any means
electronic, mechanical, photocopying, recording
or otherwise, without the prior written permission
of Wright Media Group Incorporated, First Edition 2019.
Copyright 2019 Wright Media Group Inc.
For information, Contact Special Sales Department
Wright Media Group, Inc. Philadelphia PA
(Email at: twrightmediagroup@gmail.com)

This Publisher and Author disclaim any personal liability, loss
or risk incurred as a consequence of the use and application,
either directly or indirectly, of any advice, information or
methods presented in this publication.
Printed in the United States of America

"This book of the law shall not depart out of your mouth; but you shall meditate therein day and night, that you may observe to do according to all that is written therein: for then you shall make your way prosperous, and then you shall have good success.
-(Joshua 1:8).

CONTENTS

Introduction	11	
A Thought	12	
Words to Motivate	15	
Chapter One	17	Seven Habits for Developing Deliberate Wealth
Habit 1	19	Dream Big, Use Your Imagination
Habit 2	21	Start With A Good Realistic Plan.
Habit 3	22	Prepare Yourself for Success
Habit 4	24	Be Effectively Efficient
Habit 5	25	Develop Deliberate Success
Habit 6	29	Sleep On Your Decisions
Habit 7	31	Listen to What People Are Saying
Chapter Two	35	Conclusion
About The Author	37	
Other Books By Dr. Wright	39	

DRIVEN TO SUCCEED

INTRODUCTION

Do you know what really motivates you? People are often motivated by different things. Some people are motivated by money, others by love, fame, revenge, pride, and etc. What about those people who are motivated by the *"you just watch me, I'll show you!"* attitude. Motivation comes in different shapes, sizes, forms, and colors. I guess we all have something to prove to whomever, even if it is only to ourselves. Many times we do have to prove to ourselves that we can win at something. Truth be told, you are really the only person that needs to be convinced. Bottom line here is, we all need to be motivated by something or someone. Whether its positive or negative, motivation just works.

Although negative motivation can quickly turn into discouragement if received the wrong way. This really depends on how you register any type of feedback even from haters. If you are a positive person then anything negative can be considered constructive criticism. You can turn it into some kind of motivation. An example would be, If you were a professional boxer looking to get a title fight and someone says, *"you're going to be the next champ of the world."* that would be considered positive motivation. If someone else you respected told you that *"you will never make it to become champ"* that could be turned into negative motivation. Even if it is all hate and malice you can always go with the old stand by saying, *"you just watch me, I'll show you!"*

People saying means things to you can easily be turned into motivation to propel you forward. Any kind of constructive motivation is enough to get you up and going. The best motivation is when you can encourage yourself. You have got to read everyday and study biographies of successful people. You can also watch lots of motivational videos (YouTube). The following habits are sure winners in driving you to succeed with unstoppable motivation. These habits are designed for helping you to develop deliberate wealth and overwhelming success. Enjoy the book!

A THOUGHT

They often say you have to have a better idea to succeed. This is not always true. You can find something that is already doing well and do that. There are tons of examples of people doing what you already want to do. There are biographies you can read, people you can see or hear about that are involved in doing the same thing you desire to do. I say watch and study them. Study the way these people think and conduct themselves. Notice how hard they work to achieve the results that they get. Never underestimate how much massive action is necessary to achieve your dream.

As you read this book, I want you to realize that you need others to help you along your success journey. Don't focus on money but focus on quality service, and added value. Money will come as a result of what you bring to the market place. Ninety percent of all success comes from having a great attitude. Be willing to work smart and hard. You have to get off your butt and start moving toward your goal now! When you know where you're going and what you want, the universe has a tendency to get out of your way.

Let's be totally honest with ourselves by forgetting our ego, eliminating our pride, and being willing to get down to business *right now*. Let's try our best to focus on creating a product or service of value first and then offering it to others. Condition yourself for success.

Success has to be planned and earned. The secret to this whole thing in a nutshell is, if you focus on success, wealth will always show up. If a professional boxer keeps knocking out his opponents, wealth will always follow him.

THOUGHT CONTINUED

This does not happen the other way around. Success is the generator of wealth. If you keep winning, you keep getting paid. The more success, the more pay. This also happens at work too.

Sometimes you have to qualify yourself for a raise by first doing more consistently, then you can ask for a raise later. If you keep this in mind you will always be prosperous. Don't get the order mixed up. No unsuccessful person has ever become wealthy. Whether you know it or not, people are depending on you to become successful. This is because many of them don't have the faith and motivation that you have. They see something in you to inspire them to get moving. Success is a great motivator. Success speaks louder than words.

In order to live your dreams, as Les Brown often says, you've got to first build one. If you build your dream effectively, you can then live in it.

Service to others should be your main priority when starting a business. If you go into a profession with service in mind, financial abundance won't be far behind. This unselfish thinking generates all kinds of wonderful ideas that will just pop into your head. This has happened to me so many times. Never be motivated by money when thinking of new ideas. Let service to others be your motivation

DRIVEN TO SUCCEED

WORDS TO MOTIVATE

"The more you do, the more you can do"
- Thomas Jefferson

"To get something you never had,
You've got to do something you never did"
-Denzel Washington

"Pull something out of your future and do it now."
-Steve Chandler

"It's never to late to be what you might have been"
-George Eliot

"If your ship doesn't come in, Swim out to meet it"
-Les Brown

"How you do anything, is how you do everything"
-Jack Canfield

"When it comes to infinity, you can never take more than your share"
-Bob Proctor

"We first form habits, then our habits form us"
-John Maxwell

DRIVEN TO SUCCEED

Chapter One

"Both poverty and riches are the offspring of thought"
-Neopolian Hill

The 7 Habits for Developing Deliberate Wealth starts with an abundance mindset!

If you were to change yourself you would be able to change your entire circumstance. The operative words here are *You* and *Change*. It's not the economy, it's not taxes, the industry, high prices, interest rates, or any other external factors. It's *You*! Stop making excuses and stop blaming everybody else and take full responsibility for yourself. Let's work on *You*. This is the source of the entire problem. If you would change your thinking you can change your life. If you have a job, don't dress for the job you have. Dress for the job you want. If you are not doing well in life then you have got to be willing to make massive changes in your psychology (which affects your physiology). This internal change will change everything for you. You will physically look broke in your bad disposition. People can see you coming a mile away. Your mental state has the power to shape you mentally and physically. As psychologists tell us, "Ninety percent of our communication is non verbal." When people look at you, what do they see? If poverty can be seen from a distance, so can having an Abundance Mindset. If a good idea is going to pop into your mind, it will develop within an abundance mindset and not in scarcity mode. Success ideas can happen at any moment within this abundant state.

DRIVEN TO SUCCEED

Habit #1: Dream Big, Use Your Imagination.

Do you know what you want or where you are going? You just have to imagine yourself *being* there. Try to visualize it. This cannot be just a vague thought. Take time, sit down and daydream about what you want. Then try to see it happening. As it was said earlier, in order to be a winner, you'll have to think like a winner.

Don't be afraid to imagine yourself being successful. It won't cost you a cent. Go ahead, put up those dream boards. See yourself becoming successful and wealthy. Get an image of something in your mind, use pictures you cut out of magazines, travel brochures or from the internet. And dream, dream, dream. Try and **dream big and then start small**.

You need to start imagining the possibilities of becoming successful. This has to be intrinsic before it can be manifested physically in your life. A sky-scraper building can only be built when it is finished. Before a physical building is constructed, the plans and the architectural rendering of the structure, design and layout has to be finished first. This also works for the physical manifestation of your success. You *Must* first achieve it intrinsically. You *Must* see it as a reality in your own mind first!

It is difficult to take massive action towards a dream when there is no confidence. It's like running through the forest with all of your might having your eyes closed. Eventually you're going to run into a tree or worse. You would be cautious at every move. *"Confidence is the ability along with the attitude and willingness to perform"* -Dee-Pak Chopra

Be a real leader with a vision that can be communicated to others. The Bible states that, *"As a man thinks in his heart, so is he."* Your mind leads your body. Before you can do anything it has to first become a thought. You must begin to speak positively and start feeling like you are already successful.

Sometimes, when starting out in business, it is possible to get visions of grandeur. We can be tempted to run too quickly and not cautiously in making right decisions. The thing here is to think big but start small. Let expansion happen organically when starting out in business. Never force expanding a business. Your actions have to be congruent with the vision and purpose of why you are doing what you do.

When you hear on the news of a sensational discovery or innovative product, this didn't happen overnight. It may have been publicized overnight, but it may have taken years of research and study to create the result. Some newly discovered singers call themselves, a ten year overnight sensation. A child prodigy didn't graduate from college at age 15 to become smart, He graduated at age 15 because he was already smart. Let your success first start in your mind. You succeed because you are already a success. Success is created as a result of a plan in place. Being *"Lucky"* can be defined as when opportunity meets preparation. Be prepared to do that which is necessary to become what you want. If it's more skills, education, confidence, drive or whatever, Go Get It! Your life will change when you change!

One of the biggest habits of the extremely wealthy is that they read a lot. Rich people are quick to hear and slow to speak. That's why they "know stuff". Close your mouth and open your ears. Let your learning lead to wealth. Brian Tracy believes that, *"You should work harder on yourself than you do on your job."* Study successful people by reading about them. Let the library or bookstore be your friend!

Reading is an essential ingredient to having a successful business. You will find that the more you read, the more you want to read. Reading about other successful people and the challenges they overcame to succeed will help to motivate you. Reading gives you a fresh perspective on things and more to share with others. Leaders inspire action. Read, study, change your attitude and never stop learning. Reading increases your knowledge like nothing else. Wow! Imagine that!

Habit #2: Start With A Good Realistic Plan.

You need to start with a good if not great strategy. This involves your core competency or specialty that gives you the edge over others in your business. A strategy gives you your aim and plan in order to achieve your goal. A strategy answers the question?, *why am I here, what am I trying to do, and what am I all about?* Having a good strategy starts with *Why* before it considers *How!* What is your story?

You need a game plan that will direct your endeavor. It doesn't have to be the perfect plan but good enough for it to become doable as well as feasible to execute. You don't have to spend forever planning and become so overwhelmed that you never get started. I know people who are always planning and never doing. Don't get caught up in that trap. They call it
paralysis of the analysis. Every business has a strategy. Your strategy is either a good one, or not so good one.

As they say, *a good plan executed today is better than a **great** plan executed tomorrow.* Even a good strategy may have to be revisited once in awhile to make sure it's still relevant and up to date. Chances are, your strategy may need tweaking along the way. When you enter the game you've got to have something unique and different in order for you to stand out. What is your competitive advantage? Learn to speak the customer's language. Your resources are more than you think. Look around and make an assessment of your assets, strengths, core competences, specialties and particular skills. Ask yourself, "What am I pretending not to see?"

You need to give people a good reason why they should buy from you. Be ready to give **higher** value than what you are paid. You can't give more in cash value but you can in usage value. What is your strategy for doing business? Why are you in business? Where do you stand out and what methods do you intend to use? If you have true passion for what you have to offer, you can easily answer these questions.

Habit #3: Prepare Yourself for Success, SWOT Analysis

This analysis looks at your Strengths, Weaknesses, Opportunities available to you now and possible Threats you can recognize. Make a detailed record on a piece of paper of all of your strengths. This includes all of your assets (drivers license, degrees, skills, God given gifts and talents, etc.).

Secondly, list your weaknesses. This is not to put yourself down but to help you see yourself more clearly. Admit your weaknesses to yourself. Know exactly what you are good at and what you really are bad at. Get someone to help you get to where you want to go. Find people who are good at the things that you are not good at. This helps you to keep going while eliminating road blocks. So many people stop at their own limitations. Be wise enough to ask for help. Become unstoppable like a Mack truck as people will either help you or get out of your way. With this attitude, nothing can stop you from succeeding. This allows you to keep moving forward as you focus on your strengths. Be insightful and honest enough to know when you need assistance from others. Warren Buffet says he's smart in spots, so he stays around those spots. Having insight is serious business. Insight represents understanding. The Bible says that, "...*In all of your getting, get understanding.*"[2] Know your strengths and weaknesses!

Thirdly, list your opportunities. You need to always be on the lookout for opportunities everywhere you go. There are opportunities everywhere. Lastly, be honest in listing your threats. This includes people and areas that are doing you no good. You know who and where they are. You want to maximize your opportunities and minimize your threats. You need to start moving. Once you get some kind of momentum, other ideas will pop into your head. Remember, one good idea can make you millions. The first employee of your business is *You*. Are you disciplined for growth?

7 HABITS FOR DELIBERATE WEALTH

Discipline creates freedom. Discipline yourself for success by creating and forming wealth habits. You have to have an emotional investment in what you are doing. You need discipline in handling money. Try to increase your financial acumen by reading. Having tons of money with no discipline is like driving a car at one hundred miles an hour with no steering wheel and no brakes. You're eventually going to end up in a crash. If you take a speeding locomotive off the track, where does it go? Success demands discipline. Ideas create wealth which generates money/cash flow. Also, remember to have good values and never lie about anything. Be disciplined to tell the truth and you will prosper. Not doing so is a threat to your success and reputation.

I used to rehearse being wealthy until I got good at it. This is the only way it can actually become a reality. You've got to have an unstoppable desire for your dream. Healthy and wealthy situations are created from healthy and wealthy thoughts. If a good idea is going to come into your head, it will only come when your mind is open for it. Good feelings create good thoughts. Discipline your mind to think uplifting thoughts. As we mentioned earlier, if you want to be a winner, you have to *think* like a winner. No one really fails. They just get results. Sometimes those results may not always be what we expected. Learn from those unfavorable results and make the proper changes as a result. Don't look at bad results as failure or it will attract *more* failure. Remember, *like attracts like*. What are you attracting? I'm not saying pretend that everything is great. I'm saying just don't dwell on those negative thoughts because it won't help you in becoming successful. Good ideas thrive on fertile ground. You can have the best seeds, but where they're planted is crucial. If you plant them in gravel or sand, nothing will grow. Good seeds need good soil. Good ideas are generated/revealed in the good soil of your mind.

One favorite scripture of mine is, *"....but be ye transformed by the renewing of your mind..."*[3] Stay in a positive mental state. It is crucial toward your success. Be very careful about what and how you are thinking. *Proverbs states, "The thoughts of the diligent tend only to plenteousness, but everyone that is hasty only to want."* Discipline yourself to regularly do a SWOT analysis.

Habit #4: Be Effectively Efficient

Strategy is just a part of the equation. You will also need a way to operate effectively. How is this vehicle going to run? Without good operations a strategy is just a vision. Operations is the actual work that needs to be done. You wouldn't' just get into a car or truck for the first time without checking out some of the basic features. Such as the head lights, turn signals, wind shield wipers, gas fill, and etc.

Having thorough operations in your small business allows you to start putting things in place which is very important. Don't wait for your company to grows to then start being professional. Start now while you are small. Make your service or product a high standard commodity. Have an attitude of professionalism when interacting with customers. Be a person of high integrity and great ethics. Do what you said you would do, even to your own inconvenience. Show customers that they can trust you and your word. Develop a policy of excellence. If you do all of these things, money will never be an issue.

Who is going to do *what* in your business? It is similar to a movie producer bringing everyone together and putting them in their proper places according to their roles. At the initial start, you may be wearing most of the hats but at least you will know what these hats are. Get the most essential things you really need for the business to operate effectively. It should be a service business to start, thus less overhead. Operations is simply the physical follow through of actions in your strategy (vision). It's the *how* to your *why*. Remember, a company is just a group of people. What is your *outreach*? Exactly who are you trying to reach? You are a company of one right now. It's up to you to: *Just Do It!*

Habit #5: Develop Deliberate Success and Wealth!

If becoming rich is your goal, then don't study poverty. Abraham Lincoln said, *"You can't help the poor by being one of them."*
Focus on the cure not the problem. You cannot be friends with poverty if you want to be rich. Poverty has to be your enemy. You can't love both riches and poverty. You need to hate one and cleave to the other. Remember, they are direct opposites.

If you want to help the poor, become rich. Let's face it, *"You can't help nobody if you ain't got no money!"* Do yourself and others a favor; *Become Rich!* You have got to do this for yourself and your family. Begin to operate in an abundant mentality. You can actually pay you bills with a good idea. (I have)! See poverty as a myth. The only real thing is wealth.

"Do things in life the way other people don't do them. Change the status quo, then you'll succeed." -Sheldon Adelson, (Youtube interview 2009)

TV's Shark Tank co-host Mark Cuban says that, *"You should begin to visualize your product or service as every customer or business using it. "*

You need to be honest with yourself and ask, "What would wealth give me that I don't already have?" If it is just a feeling, then you need to start feeling wealthy now! All of the money in the world is spent on feeling good. Not having money is a disgrace and an embarrassment. Being without and in need is down right humiliating. Put it in your head that being prosperous is in God's plan for you. It's all up to you to feel successful. You need to begin to feel like a winner before you can actually become one. Years ago when I didn't have a penny to my name, no one knew it by looking at me. I carried myself with a wealth mentality. Only your disposition and attitude can give your situation away. I've always walked like a winner. This is how I started becoming successful. Being poor isn't cool, so get with the program. There are approximately 36 million millionaires in the world and according to Forbes magazine, there are 1,542 billionaires too. Most of them are entrepreneurs. This proves that there is no shortage of wealth. Abundance is everywhere!

You need to begin to set a higher standard for yourself today. Prepare your mind to jump into the flow of abundance. If you were about to jump into a stream, it won't stop moving and wait until you get in. You'll just have to jump into the flow and such is life. The ocean is not like a bus that stops and waits for you to hop on. It never stops moving. It flows 24 hours a day and 7 days a week. Thus, success is not in short supply it's like an ocean. As Jim Rohn said in his Youtube 2007 motivational speech, *"Some people go to the ocean with a teaspoon. They should trade it in for a bucket. They'll look better down at the ocean, and kids won't make fun of them."* I truly believe that the only limits people have are the ones they place on themselves. I have a good friend who is totally blind, yet he runs a television network and several restaurants. He truly has vision. He is a millionaire. In his younger years as a blind person, people had often suggested that he get a box and beg on the streets. He refused and rejected the idea because he knew of the greatness within himself.

It's up to you to save your own little world and come to your own rescue. Author Grant Cardone states, *"Being Wealthy is your Duty, Obligation and Responsibility"*. That's why you need to be *driven to succeed!* If you change your words, you'll change your world. Stop begging for opportunities and create your own. Watch what you say when you talk to yourself and others. Don't try and talk yourself out of a good idea. Focus on what you can do *now*.

Give yourself the gift of time. Command your actions verbally. Go after opportunities don't wait for them to come to you. Stop looking for easy things or trying to get something for nothing.

"Don't search for opportunity in the distance but recognize them right where you are" -(Napoleon Hill, Think & Grow Rich).

NOTES

Habit #6: Sleep On Your Decisions.

In business, there will always be difficult decisions to make. However, there will also be difficult decisions that really don't have to be made right away. Don't be afraid to sleep on a decision. You'll be surprised what the next day will bring. If what you are about to do in your business has a chance of failing and you know you will not be able to recover financially, then don't do it until you are sure. I like calculated risks better than gambling. A calculated risk prepares for contingencies. Gambling does not. Be wise in business and be careful when making decisions. Never put yourself in a *go for broke* situation. As they say, don't put all of your eggs in one basket, If you do, then watch that basket like a hawk.

Make yourself responsible for your money. Study how rich people think. You don't need more money. You need more *ideas*. You need a real money making machine idea or a cash-cow concept. You need the power to get wealthy, not a bunch of get rich gimmicks thrown at you. Remember what I said earlier. Undisciplined money won't solve your money problems, Your mind solves money problems. You need to learn how to master your thinking so you can master your money and generate cash flow. Develop your mind in areas of handling money wisely. Create something important that the world really needs instead of thinking about how to get big really fast. Your world represents the people around you. Be a person of purpose and drive. Your subconscious mind will try and make these things happen for you too. You will be guided toward successful ideas. You need to stay up to date and informed concerning new technologies and what's coming next. I heard it said that readers are leaders. I read and study tons of information and am able to recall most of it, thanks to memory techniques. Remember, each decision you make as a new entrepreneur is crucial. A bad decision will affect your business and your confidence. Take your time whenever making decisions and sleep on it first!

NOTES

7 HABITS FOR DELIBERATE WEALTH

Rule #7: Listen to What People Are Saying

Listen to what people are saying about your business. If you hear the same things two or three times, take note. Let your customers or even potential customers help you to help them. Listen to what they are saying about your product or service. Some film actors and directors enjoy going to the theater along with moviegoers, just to hear the audience's true reaction to their films. In order to stay in business, you must hear the truth. This will help you to make adjustments in how to best serve your customers. If you hear people with the same complaints about your business, then use the feedback to correct things. If you hear the same compliments, then do more of that.

Are you excited and convinced that what you are selling is definitely something you would use yourself. Is it something people really need or want? It has to be something that will add a true benefit to those who purchase it. Even if you decided to open up a street car wash, make sure you are giving the best possible service ever. Give great value and benefit. A little kindness and respect to all customers goes a long way too. Give customers the king or queen treatment. Make them feel good about stopping and getting their car washed at your location. Make sure you do an exceptional job so they would want to come back again and again. Remember, you are not just making a sale, you are making a customer. You should be thinking long term relationship with every customer that patronizes your business. As it is said, you only get one chance to make a first impression, so make it a good one!

There is nothing wrong with developing a win/win relationship with a customer. No one has to be the loser in any of your business transactions. Society tells us that someone has to lose. In his book, *The Seven Habits of Highly Effective People,* Steven Covey reminds us that a win/win situation can be achieved. Covey says that you have to *"Begin with the end in mind and know how you want your meeting or presentation to go."* In essence he is saying to *see the end in the very beginning"*. Create something of true value first, then offer it to potential customers. Show up with service to the customer in mind and begin to think about what the customer needs and wants. A good rule would be to under promise and over deliver. There are some people that will tell you to go through the door without the answer and when you get under pressure, you'll discover the answer. I don't believe in jumping out of a window and learning to fly on the way down. That's called suicide. I like being prepared because it helpsbuild confidence.

I believe as an entrepreneur that you should always give customers more than they expect. It needs to be about the customer first. Think of how you can serve them better. Listening is also the key. Remember, sales is like a ping pong game. There has to be even exchange, thus win/win. Sell with passion and integrity. Begin to think outside of yourself. Put yourself in the shoes of the customer. Business should capture a customers heart, not just their pocket book. Think of winning a customer, not just a sale. Know that you must give value to receive value.

Demand integrity from yourself. Learn to put everything you've got into anything you do. Don't think you need to save something for later. Believe me, later will have another set of benefits and values you can offer to new customers. When you sell using inspiration, good feelings, and passion, they will buy from you without buyers remorse. People love feeling good about their decisions. You are actually selling good feeling centered around your product or service. What can you give of value first to attract customers? You will be entering the law of cause and affect. Whatever you send out comes back. Listen, listen, listen to your customers as often as possible.

Selling anything is easy if you are convinced that it will make a difference in people's lives. The better you get at it, the more money you will make. Look at it as you are helping people and doing them a favor. Whatever you have, be it product, service, or concept, sell it with passion and purpose. Have a true mission and purpose. If you have a viable mission, energy will be present. Be first class with it and present it from your heart. You can persuade, inspire, and influence customers, without using manipulation. *"If what you are offering is good, people will tell others. They will shout about it."* -Jeff Bezos– Amazon founder.

Work with all of your strength, be diligent and experience the blessing. I heard someone say, *"It will work if you work it!"*
The good feelings of your enjoyment will resonate to every customer.

People DO want to feel good when they are purchasing something. As I heard someone once say, *"Sell the sizzle, not just the steak."* Selling something is the only way for you to get rich. I recommend that you learn how to sell and find a product or service that you believe in and that fits your personality. You must be people oriented in order to survive and make your business work. You should make it your habit to constantly seek criticism. Don't be afraid of the truth. You Can Handle It!

NOTES

Chapter Two

CONCLUSION:

"It's not your fault if you were born poor, but It is your fault if you die poor".

- Daniel Ally

These practical habits are just the beginning. This book's subtitle does mention *Wealth, and Success*. These appear to be the same, however, they are not. Wealth is moving forward with no particular state of emotion. It could be summed up as cash flow. Success is an internal feeling or state of being. It is a state of mind derived from fulfillment. The combination of them both is being in balance and congruent with each other. It is possible to be wealthy without feeling successful. Success gives wealth meaning. Inherited wealth needs meaning attached to it. This is why so many wealthy people become philanthropists, give to charities or start foundations. Now that you have completed this reading, use the information in this book as a reference. Refer to it often. Keep these 7 habits close for continued guidance. I already know you are now Driven to Succeed with Unstoppable Motivation. Congratulations and continued SUCCESS!

NOTES

ABOUT THE AUTHOR

Dr. Titus C. Wright is a motivational speaker, expert sales trainer, business & biology professor, and CEO of Wright Media Group. He is the inspired author of *How To Get The Man/Woman of Your Dreams, Waiting To Be Great, Forced To Be Rich* and *Why You Should Be Rich.* Titus motivates thousands of people per week with his *Positive Force* Youtube videos, magazine publications, and self help books. He is blessed to have earned two Masters degrees in business administration/management. He also received a doctorate (Ph.D.) in Christian Education. Titus has dedicated his life to personal self development and in helping others find their true purpose and passion. He has appeared on local and national television shows, numerous radio programs and in newsprint/magazines. He lives in Pennsylvania with his lovely wife, Coral.

DRIVEN TO SUCCEED is Titus's seventh nationwide book release. It is said by many that his books are worth their weight in *Pure Gold*. His multi-media organization continues to thrive due to these God-given habits. He adheres to his own advice and has been able to implement these concepts in his own life and business. Titus believes that, prosperity isn't about owning things. It's about nothing owning you!

Contact email: twrightmediagroup@gmail.com

Available for corporate and academic speaking engagements.

DRIVEN TO SUCCEED

Other Books By Dr. Titus C. Wright

Get Your Copy Today! One of a Kind Books From
The #1 Motivated Author: Dr. Titus C. Wright

AMAZON.COM/TITUS C. WRIGHT

Business Success

ALL NEW! TITLES!

Relationship Success

How To Get The Woman Of Your Dreams
& Man of Your Dreams

Two, One of a Kind Books That Every Person Should Have In Their Personal Collection

www.ingramcontent.com/pod-product-compliance
Lightning Source LLC
Chambersburg PA
CBHW072306170526
45158CB00003BA/1203